arson

Michael Twist is the author of *Highs & Lows*, a rare and thoughtful book which challenges perceptions of diabetes. His other poetry books include *Fireworks*, *Orbit*, *Smoke and Earth*, and *Dozen*. He lives in Vancouver, Canada.

michaeltwist.com

ISBN 978-0-9879415-3-4

Jellyfish

michaeltwist.com

Printed in Canada.

arson

Jellyfish

...Cautiously let us step into the era of the unchained fire.

– Milosz

CONTENTS

Acknowledgements   *x*

Five Minutes   2

Whispers   4

Deluge   5

Sand Surf Tide   8

Present Perfect   10

True Friend   14

Commotion   16

Minefield   18

Homeless   20

No Fixed Address   24

Hive   26

Arson   28

Deafening   30

CONTENTS

Mute Crows   34

Mirror   36

Opaque   38

Vitals   40

Charity   43

Sparrow   45

Magic 8 Ball   47

Jump Ship   50

Publishing Pirates   52

Last Laugh   55

A Steal   57

Lost Keys   59

On Remembering   60

Che's Way   62

Still Reeling   63

Renovation   65

Acknowledgements

Arson is dedicated to Rod Paul Martin who had a way with words and lived his passion.

> *When near your death a friend*
> *Asked you what he could do,*
> *'Remember me', you said.*
> *We will remember you.*
>   *– Thom Gunn*

Thanks to Rosalind for reviewing early drafts of *Arson*.

This book is also for poets who keep the fires burning.

Five Minutes

If I had time

I'd compose misty showers:

abrupt clouds agitated

by bracing breath

over the damp after-rain sheen

of expectant city streets.

I'd compose fathomless oceans:

vast volumes of wave and tide

replete with stretching starfish

creeping over crags

peppered with barnacles;

salty sea kisses.

I'd compose a struggling man:

possession-laden,

hastily animated,

involved downtown

in anxious bustle,

now jaywalking.

I'd compose somnambulists:

commuters emerging en masse

from a gaping aperture in the ground each day;

women open umbrella umbilici,

clutch movable shelters.

I'd compose a ruffled janitor:

world-weary,

sweeping remainders;

yesterday's trees.

I'd write because I had five minutes.

Whispers

On the cusp

a shift happens

before long.

Confused clouds alter,

clandestine storms spin in a darkening dusk.

Moisture permeates humid air,

grasp it with fragile fingers,

bones and flesh—

we are mere whispers,

light rain in Spring.

Deluge

Our prefab,

tinfoil world

rewards the affluent—

The rest struggle,

try forging a life from fragments

fused together,

infinite pieces of stained glass.

Held against light

shards glisten;

cast colours through darkness.

Fragments may sever

slick smooth surfaces,

happy hues

disguise the scalpel,

reassurances it will be painless.

Guilt an infinite ocean;

the deluge came.

We joked about the flood—

who wouldn't?

When it seemed a mere drizzle

the river soon spilled over,

assaulted the plain.

Downtown all clear

despite disaster,

people shuffle to work amidst the flood

while the affluent sleep

with dreams

impending catastrophe.

Rising water levels go unnoticed,

warnings not to drink the water ignored—

Who builds arks anymore?

Sand Surf Tide

These days spent

in suspended animation.

Jungle hindrance:

impenetrable growth impedes

hunt machete-wielding

chop passageways

search for doors.

How many hours

scalded in a bath of sunshine?

Cringe on entering the sea,

wind turns tides,

forms rocks from the fray,

directs ocean swells.

To be, to be this sea,

fill the Earth sated in flux,

crash waves on crushed-coral beaches,

delight in all creatures living

within you, break on rocks,

make whirlpools

around crags and cliffs,

your dream to be the sea!

We need Triton more than ever;

oceans and skies and trees

in which to believe.

Present Perfect

Have you seen imploding windows?

Have you feared to face the day?

Are you happy where you are

or could you see another way?

Have you spoken with a Muslim?

Have you interviewed a Jew?

Have you chatted with a stranger

and learned a lesson too?

Have you eaten tasty sushi?

Have you tried to go off meat?

Have you wondered how a farmer

raised the food you eat?

Have you learned another language?

Have you travelled far and wide?

Have you ended looking outward

and tried looking deep inside?

Have you complained about the weather?

Have you grumbled about your car?

Have you headed for the grocery store

and stopped off in a bar?

Have you dwelt on the past?

Have you forgotten about today?

Have you wanted something so very much

you scared it right away?

Have you broken something pricey?

Have you felt extremely proud?

Have you tried to be more subtle

and come off way too loud?

Have you called yourself a poet?

Have you suffered for your art?

Have you faced a blank page

without knowing where to start?

Have you held your breath for minutes?

Have you had your face turn blue?

Have you got a nasty notice

that the money owed is due?

Have you done the crossword?

Have you finished another book?

If someone stopped to check you out

would you turn to take a look?

Have you changed the world?

Have you lived your life?

Did you have a husband?

Did you have a wife?

Are you living life for now

or for a distant past?

Share your experience

and by sharing, make it last.

True Friend

Fireball,

you willingly share

heat and light,

appear skyward

marking mornings

with orange hues.

Like an old friend

you keep company,

smile warmly,

set colour afire—

You demand

no toilsome bargains,

no deadlines, ask

for no edits;

you make your way across the sky,

quietly gargantuan,

gaseous substances blazing.

You radiate energy

without expectation,

shine without debts owed,

a true friend indeed.

Commotion

Perhaps I contemplate too much

for my own good,

but then who am I to judge?

I've been like this all my life;

a temperament incessantly considering

the timbre of sound,

the rush of tires on pavement

the concentration of rainfall.

Who can judge the clouds

swirling slowly with their grey moods?

They were forming ephemeral shapes

long before you and me.

The overwhelming instrument of concrete city

turns nature into faceless streets

on which we travel,

windshield wipers

sweep raindrops away

with unobscured vision

relocate towards a future finish.

Make the journey pleasant,

like perpetual imperceptible breathing

in the crushing commotion

before awakening to a new day.

Minefield

Tread carefully

through the everyday,

mind the gap

between your beliefs and actions

and how the world works.

Storms arise,

threatening to knock you down,

choose battles among many.

Watch people act out

the same role,

live their lives,

like anesthetized robots,

board and alight bloated buses.

And again

yet again find themselves

out of time.

Homeless

His wild eyes may not take you in,

like a skid row junkie disheveled;

worn out,

had enough days,

fed up though unfed.

He counts carefully collected empties in his cart,

drowns in rattling wheels,

folds away his dreams carefully,

packing dirty laundry.

He sleeps tonight

beside the beauty salon

where ladies get their hair done.

He wraps himself in plaid blankets,

touches wet pavement with fingers

that once touched a girl.

Before and after;

sudden switch,

so we'd like to believe.

We crave

simple solutions,

hypodermic answers

quick crack narratives.

We crave

lives resolved

in a neat wrapped package;

pretty paper

ribbons and bows

cover the corpse.

Where are the witnesses?

Where are the mutineers?

Disasters dominate confused headlines,

class ruptures delineated by affordable alleys,

political poverty's impotent discourse.

Cars provide protection

against the blood-stained day,

avoiding the burial of the living dead,

convince ourselves it's not so bad.

Could be a lot worse.

Tomorrow's paper will come with hollow headlines

he'll use to line the bottom of the box,

another layer insulates from the cold street.

No wonder he became

a sidewalk astronaut;

he took one small step,

then stepped off

alit the bus,

told culture to stuff it.

At the watering hole,

SUVs gather guzzling gas.

The bus nears my stop,

a few more lurches

and I'll be home,

stepping into the rain,

a broken man falling apart at the seams,

threadbare and worn.

No Fixed Address

To those transitioning,

in-between, limbo-living:

who needs a fixed address?

Ties down to the ground

so roots grow,

strangling materially;

detach entangled possessions,

deadweights drag.

The road beckons;

trials materialize along its dusty back,

unintended destinations,

disruptions, astonishment

and tedium,

such a long route stretches

into the distance,

twists and turns interminably.

Tiring trip worth footsteps,

every worn backpack lug,

every leg protest.

Live the journey and go,

go away

learn yourself.

Hive

Honey home of hive

buzzes with busy design,

a complex

combined effort.

Sweet syrup,

sticky and strong

seduces the tongue

with its amber glow.

Who could know this slowly finished gold,

this shimmering sugar embedded

inside honeycombs

contained sating sunshine?

These grids of abode

assembled by

a droning multitude,

abuzz and intoxicating

build paper cathedrals,

their holy hum.

Arson

Write language on fire,

burning poets rage.

Words possess combustible wicks

lit quickly to flame,

just as rapidly

beckon bewilderment.

Incendiary author as arsonist,

scorching ideas with burning questions,

each pen flick sets pages on fire

and yes, they smolder

as we all burn.

Like a phoenix

words arise again from ashes,

something from nothing,

nothing to one.

With a bit of luck,

ideas emerge intact from this forge,

enflame anew.

Words like lightning ignite the sky,

their wildfire rushes lush forests.

Deafening

Wind forces clouds across the sky,

propositions the summer end go ignored,

broken truces blow about.

Children storm the barricades,

their wails and shrieks

echoing park-bound

bring the wind to deafening.

Toddlers teeter, meet the ground

with tumbles and tripping,

they have not yet become spectres

of dying summer.

Wind like blood courses

its atmospheric circulation,

its demand and impatience,

rushes and ebbs.

Sun makes for glowing embers,

like this dusk-drowned park,

ruddy hues take over the day.

The wind alarm

storms my face:

go, it says.

Days pass like molasses,

slow and steady,

seeping through sleeping hours,

sloth-like distraction from current reminders.

Wind language

lives in us:

go, it whispers,

go to the day.

For the children,

blockades must fall;

knock down the fences!

I never had a home to go to,

the house which holds the hearth;

receptacle of dream combustion.

Thought got you there

we think, though Descartes

tripped up, like Newton examining

pebbles on his seashore, left us

with too many egos.

(You can make the numbers

say anything)

they bend to wills.

I lived there,

I live and go,

Revel in the sheer joy of go.

Mute Crows

Time never one

to give an inch—

won't budge on the bus

or slow its hasty pace.

Crows squawk and caw,

in treetop argument,

finding words among branches

and green growth,

they settle the issue then

take flight.

Sometimes I wander past

late at night,

and in the same tree they pause,

a couple of crows mute

in the coming blackness.

They disappear into

dark surroundings,

they stare with

shiny black capsules,

their brittle beaks

peck everything raw.

Mirror

Still searching

for the man behind the curtain,

the pusher of buttons,

the head honcho.

Look harder;

search the heavens to find him

among clouds.

He lost his umbrella,

ran out of cigarettes this morning,

forgot his keys.

His insomnia interrupted

with dreams of smooth spirits,

shapeless in early hours

before awakening.

Look carefully

for the person who stares back at you

from the broken mirror each morning.

Opaque

Between every good morning

empty paper cups expect makeshift breakfasts

eaten too hastily,

embittered coffee bites my tongue.

Atypical day doctor-bound,

I join the onlookers en route.

A wrinkled face sits in his time,

clutching his chest as firefighters

(serving with pride since 1886)

resuscitate from the brink.

A woman ambles past,

addressing the air,

an Alberta license plate strapped to her back.

Through car exhaust and metered parking,

a girl rides her bicycle,

a face mask protects against

dirty air.

Time slows to the fifties

in an abstract

sun-deprived waiting room

with evocative deer paintings,

forgotten plastic sunflowers,

and yesterday's magazines scattered about.

An orange seat crunches

when I sit,

over the counter

curved glass I can't

see through.

Vitals

Paramedics sip coffee,

crowd around a tiny table,

coolly lean back in chairs

while ambulances parked

in front of the café

await calamity.

They discuss

how to take vitals,

wrist or neck pulse?

Fresh fire chief

with burning questions.

Latest patients in ICU and EMERGE

lack

a 21-year-old stabbing victim

they debate cracking his chest,

how his ribs broke while kneading lungs

and heart,

he flat-lined.

Day   night   graveyard   shift

resurrected,

arising with ODs,

gang stabbings or shooting victims.

Determine too much or too little meds,

ineffective ambulance ergonomics

in critical situations.

miniscule moment

between life and death,

too late—

Nervous silence sudden,

the coffees go cold.

A radio crackles to life

and they rise.

Sirens soon wail like mourners,

advanced life support unit

navigates the traffic ebb and flow

they go.

Rushing towards resurrection

the next worrisome din.

Charity

Life in shadows,

sand for dinner,

sing to air, connect

the dots in ink-spattered specks,

music of wind and wave and rustle,

as armies advance on the horizon.

Sleep at your peril!

Awake, you may find

some solace in your life;

you may stem the approaching tide.

This monied military takes

the hills, destroys wilderness like beasts,

gorges on lush loam.

Scales tipped by

unmeasured accounts,

human sacrifice and charity;

what have you given?

Sparrow

Slow burn seeps in,

early sun stretches,

awakens

creeping across the icy morning.

A threat,

this puzzle piece cannot fit,

the outsider disconnected:

a silent sparrow sleeps,

motionless in its moment,

awaiting discovery

on the pavement

beneath the patio chair.

It may have escaped notice,

as its friends chirp cheerily;

plump beige birds hop,

jerkily moving their tiny heads,

diminutive beacons of song

search for crumbs.

An inanimate sparrow:

the coffee shop employee

unceremoniously

discards it.

Magic 8 Ball

Fingers bead blood;

daily pinprick incisions

test blood sugar levels.

Meticulously plotting

graphs of fluctuating

results:

suffering undulation.

Falling, gasping,

heart fluttering,

pace percolating with syrupy blood,

danger in sweetness and lack thereof,

prescribed defence against complications,

come what will;

ride the tide,

surf the waves.

Frequent incongruity,

immune response

tripped, multiplied

divided, destroyed

unexplained reactions,

cell implosion.

Each day often

I pluck a plastic strip

to test,

prime my finger well,

slake the mechanical vampire.

Its impromptu decision made,

like a magic 8 ball,

displays its result.

Snapshot:

sudden now.

No future prediction.

Jump Ship

Sinking ships feared,

the bends affect morning

choices hatched fresh and new,

latent taste on your tongue.

You dwell in the rind

of your skin,

peeled like lemon.

Awaken to nautical decisions

made on the fly,

pull up anchor,

turn the boat seaward

navigate to a distant shore,

but will the ship endure

seasick swells?

Jump ship and

find new quarters,

leave the husk behind,

sail off with the fruit.

Publishing Pirates

Words swim a mammoth sea

like fish.

When angling for a bite,

drift awhile;

see where the current takes you.

Submerge yourself for shellfish.

Diving for an oyster or two would suffice,

find a pearl if you're lucky.

Beware the ominous trawlers,

their immense nets full of flapping words,

plunder the sea of everything,

it's published,

shiver me timbers,

discordant and jumbled,

according to the captain's whim.

Why blame the captain?

It's all about business,

pirates have always pillaged.

What of the profiteers?

Those buccaneers evade taxes through shrewd deals

and pile plundered loot in banks offshore.

Word fisheries

depleted,

now they're farming salmon

and subsidies create local stock.

Dive deeper to find pearls,

though they may be buried beneath,

hidden in the seaweed.

Shells of abalone await

jewels for the taking rest on the ocean floor.

In murky depths luminous fish,

blinded by light

may be discovered;

rare iridescent beings

emerge from darkness.

Fish for words,

you may just catch a kettleful

Last Laugh

Majestic cedars

creak, wind-worn.

Slow water along rivers

runs its course, slips

over stones, mixes

minerals and matter, tastes

edges of Douglas Firs

quenches thirsty roots

by night.

Lightning sets alight the forest fabric,

tinder stick cedars destroyed by flickering flame,

while shadows dance, leave their

glowing embers to singe the floor,

the burning blaze razes bare.

Pine needles rain

on a park picnic table,

stars await sunrise,

slow cool dawn

extends its term.

New shoots rise,

bred from blackened earth,

bursting forth from ashes

renewed,

tender emerald infants

laugh.

A Steal

Will: $129

(Seniors $99)

what a deal.

Buy a box of lawyer

cut-price.

Uncontested divorce from only $350,

request a quote if contested.

House purchase: $275

(With mortgage $475)

Moments running on a lifetime river,

each stage,

price tag marked.

If only homes were for sale,

buy it at a bargain

to live a discounted life,

the money never mattered.

Only $129 buried.

If only death could be so inexpensive,

life's complex collection of moments left behind

priceless.

Lost Keys

The keys buried in passing years

unlock doors long forgotten

in dusty corridors,

cobwebs form.

Someone should open the window,

create a palpable escape route,

as fresh air may dispel some dust,

but the doors remain unopened,

locked unless the lost keys are found.

How easily we forget our keys,

left in an empty room

with a covered desk

and empty chair.

On Remembering

How painful is the remembering:

good times had and gone,

struggles and the leaving,

the will to carry on.

How painful it must have been:

a shocking first breath into

a blinding new world—

a panic of light and substance and sound.

These hours of song and light,

this jubilant affair,

our joyful day turned night.

What is colour but light?

A surface illusion,

persistent, painful.

This forgetful morning,

rising sun anew, existing,

and how for many hours,

this burning star persists.

Che's Way

Che said you have to do it now,

because the future is promised to no one.

The future?

A dream beyond clouds,

over mountains on an island somewhere.

No guaranteed reward at the end of it,

no trophy to collect,

no medal to pin on your lapel,

no chorus of angels,

the lights at the end of the tunnel.

Here you are,

now clear water shimmering on a sunny day,

what to do?

Still Reeling

The month arrived

too early, crashing

the party with a blizzard,

howling wind, blowing snow

into the house, making

a fool of itself, sure

it was a little tipsy, but someone

should have told it

to chill out, simmer

down, watch a bit of championship bowling

on TV, buy a Lord's Prayer cross

for $29.95, but instead

it hurled itself about,

left us all

reeling—

at the end of a long year,

told us where to

stuff our Silent Night,

glitter and Jolly St. Nick,

then like a whirlwind,

stumbled away, off

to where snow drifts as dry

and fine as sand.

Renovation

Can I renovate the day?

Put out the sun like a smoldering cigarette?

Dismantle the trees into boxes,

put away the leaves,

and send them away in letters?

Rig things in reverse:

Put back oil deposits in the ground, spread

strip-mined ores, glue

trees back onto their clear-cut stumps, paste

precious metals into rock , stick

birds back in the sky, hatch

schools of fish, let

factories leech their poison back from the rivers, inhale

their pollution from the air.

Can I roll up the roads and sidewalks, dismantle

the city buildings of glass and concrete, return

cars to elements, translate

this city to pristine nature?

www.ingramcontent.com/pod-product-compliance
Lightning Source LLC
LaVergne TN
LVHW091208080426
835509LV00006B/895